Times Change

At Work

Long Ago and Today

Lynnette R. Brent

Heinemann Library
Chicago, Illinois

Long Ago

Imagine that it is long ago. You have been at work five hours already, and it is only lunchtime! The bell rings to let everyone know that it is time for your half hour lunch break. You gladly put down the shirt you are sewing to take a much needed break.

You would rather be at school, but you know it is important to your family that you work. The money you earn helps pay for food and clothing.

This is what your life may have been like if you lived in the United States about 100 years ago. Let's see what other workers may have been doing in the United States long ago.

Children worked in factories, like this stocking factory, to help support their families.

Working People

Long ago, there were many **immigrants** entering the country. Many of them moved to large cities to look for work. Many farmers were also moving away from the country to work in the city.

Women were starting to work outside the home. However, the pay for women was lower than for men. Children as young as seven years old were also working to help support their families.

With help from adults, these children worked cleaning oysters.

Times Change

What Changed in 1938?

In 1938, the Fair Labor Standards Act set a minimum wage for children. It also said a child must be 16 years of age to work full-time.

In the United States, children are no longer found in the work place.

Today, men and women work in the same types of jobs for equal pay. Children younger than 14 years old are no longer allowed to work full-time jobs. Teenagers who work have limited hours they are allowed to work.

Wages

Although workers made less money long ago, food and goods cost much less.

Long ago, the average worker made $12.98 per week. Workers worked about 59 hours each week. A loaf of bread cost around 5 cents, and a gallon of milk cost about 25 cents.

Today, the average worker in the United States earns $584.28 per week. Workers work about 40 hours each week. A loaf of bread costs about $1.00, and a gallon of milk costs about $2.50.

Today, items may cost more, but workers bring home more money each week.

Types of Jobs

Manual labor for blue-collar workers often meant long, tiring days.

Long ago, most workers were "blue-collar," or people who worked with their hands. Blue-collar jobs included craftspeople, laborers, farmers, and miners.

A smaller group of workers were "white-collar." These included managers, salespeople, doctors, and lawyers. Women did not work in these jobs.

Today, there are more white-collar workers than blue-collar workers in the United States.

Today, most workers are white-collar workers who work as salespeople or in offices.

Fewer workers are blue-collar workers. They work in factories or in construction. Others work as cooks and cashiers. Today, women work in blue-collar and white-collar jobs.

Job Training

Young men training to be firefighters rode with experienced firefighters.

Long ago, men prepared for work by doing an **apprenticeship** for a trade. To become a firefighter, a man needed to work at the fire station and practice the skills he would need on the job.

White-collar jobs also offered apprenticeships. Workers were trained by someone in their same field. Most people did not go to college.

Today, workers train to prepare for work. This may include college courses, technical schools, or apprenticeships. To become a firefighter today, a man or woman must take college courses and then work at the fire station as an apprentice.

White-collar jobs usually require college courses. Apprenticeships are also common.

These firefighters are learning life-saving skills to prepare them for their jobs.

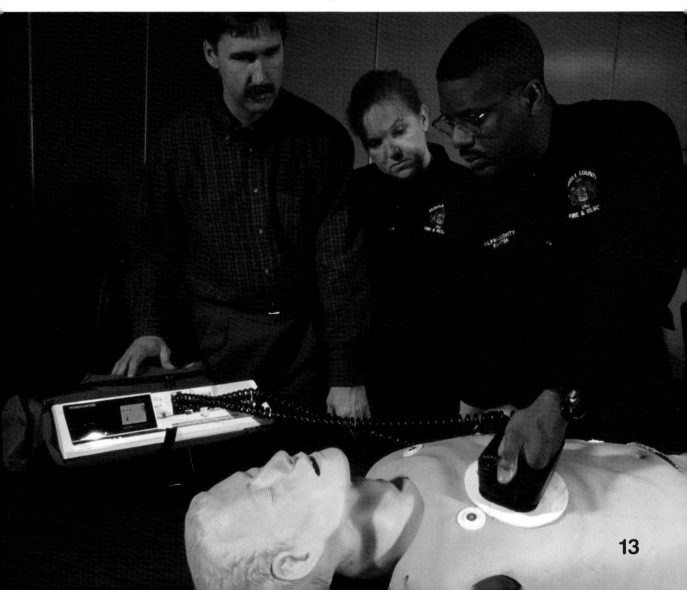

Goods and Services

Long ago, most people made things in small shops or factories. These goods included shoes, clothes, and furniture.

A small number of people provided services for others by doing something for them. Some examples include house cleaning and caring for children.

Workers in print shops like this one provided books for people.

Today, most people work to provide services for others. Some examples include teachers, plumbers, and mechanics. Many companies use machines to make goods. People are needed only to run the machines. A very small number of people make goods by hand today.

People who work in restaurants provide a service by serving food to people.

Craftspeople and Factory Workers

It took a long time for craftspeople like these to paint faces on dolls.

Long ago, craftspeople learned trades through **apprenticeships.** These included **blacksmiths,** glassblowers, **tailors,** dressmakers, and weavers. One person did the work mainly with hand tools. This made the work slow and careful.

Times Change

What Changed in the Early 1900s?

In the early 1900s, companies began using assembly lines. On an assembly line, each worker added one part to a product. More items were made at a faster pace.

Companies were able to produce more goods in less time with the use of assembly lines.

Toys that are all exactly the same are now produced quickly on machines.

Today, there are very few craftspeople left because of **automated** machines at factories. Most of our clothing, toys, and other goods come from factories or mills. Machines rather than people often assemble and produce items. Today, machines can produce hundreds of items in a shorter amount of time.

Farming Work

Long ago, most people lived on farms. Farm families raised animals and crops to support themselves. They produced meat, vegetables, and milk. Even children helped plow fields, tend to chores, and take care of the animals. Most of the food people ate came from the crops they harvested.

Long ago, everyone in the family did their fair share of the farm work.

Today, farming is treated as a business instead of a way of life. Farmers usually focus on one sort of farming, such as dairy, wheat, barley, or corn. They sell their produce to markets. It is then delivered all over the country and even the world. Most farms are owned by large businesses rather than individual families.

Today, businesses hire people to work on farms.

Getting to Work

The first street cars were pulled by horses.

Long ago, most people rode horses, rode in a buggy or wagon, or walked to work. Streetcars were becoming popular. By 1909, more people could afford to buy cars. People purchased cars for **commuting** to work.

Times Change

What Changed in 1904?

In 1904, New York City's first subway system opened. This allowed workers to travel farther from home to work each day.

New York City's first subway had 9.1 miles of track.

Today, most people drive their cars to work. Others take buses, trains, and subways, which are underground railways. Some still walk or may ride a bicycle.

Today, so many people commute to work that traffic jams are common.

The Workday

Long ago, people worked six or even seven days a week. The average workweek was 60 to 70 hours. The workday normally started around six in the morning and would last until around six in the evening. Factory workers were given very few breaks and only half an hour for lunch.

People in this glass factory worked many hours, even on Saturdays.

Today most people's workday ends around 5:00 P.M.

Today, people usually work about 40 hours a week. However, some people work more hours than that. Some people can set the hours of their workday and some even work from home.

A normal business day is eight in the morning until five in the afternoon with a one hour lunch break. Many places are open all night, so some people work late at night.

A Break from the Workday

Long ago, workers were given a half hour or sometimes an hour for lunch. Workers brought lunch with them to work in cloth napkins or in lunch buckets. Workers would eat in a small room or outside if the weather was nice. Many workers tried to take a short nap during their break.

Since people worked long hours, they would eat lunch outside as often as possible for fresh air.

Today, workers still bring their lunches to work. Some people buy food from the business's cafeteria. Sometimes people eat in a restaurant, or bring food back from a fast-food restaurant or food mart. Workers eat in a lunchroom, at their desks, or outside.

Today, workers often eat
lunch in the cafeteria.

Office Equipment and Machinery

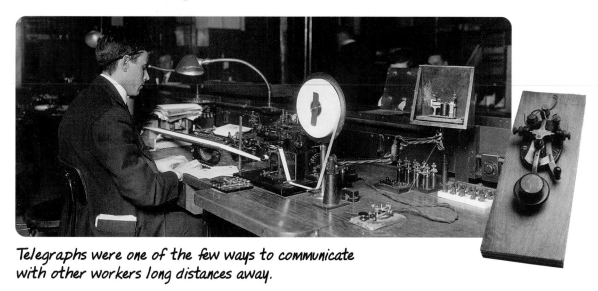

Telegraphs were one of the few ways to communicate with other workers long distances away.

Long ago, pens, paper, pencils, and typewriters were commonly used in offices. Most files were handwritten and stored in boxes or cabinets. Most communication was done by mail. Postal workers delivered the mail, first on horseback, and later in mail trucks. **Telegraphs** and **telegrams** were also used but were more expensive than mailing a letter.

Times Change

What Changed in 1977?

In 1977, Apple Computers introduced the Apple II. This successful personal computer was inexpensive and simple to use. Many companies bought them for people to use at work.

The Apple II computer quickly became a common piece of equipment in the workplace.

Technology has made communication quicker and easier.

Today, businesses use equipment like telephones, fax machines, and computers to communicate. Sending e-mails is very common. Many important files are stored on computer disks or on the computer. Trucks, planes, and trains deliver regular mail from one place to another.

Workers' Rights

Workers went on strike to ask for better working conditions.

Long ago, workers had few rights in the workplace. Companies would not pay workers who took time off for illness or family emergencies. Many companies would replace them with someone else. If workers were injured at work, they had to pay for treatment on their own. **Health insurance** was not provided.

Times Change

What Changed in the 1910s?

By the 1910s, workers were joining unions in order to get better pay, shorter work hours, and safer, cleaner work places.

Unions formed to fight for the rights of workers.

Today, workers have more job security. They are allowed time off if they or someone in their family has an emergency or is sick. Workers would receive pay for this time off. If workers are injured on the job, the company pays for their treatment. Health insurance is often offered at the workplace. Most businesses offer paid vacation time.

Working conditions are safer and cleaner today.

You have seen how work has changed in the last 100 years. One hundred years ago, you may have been working instead of going to school. Today, children go to school and adults work.

Long ago, adults sometimes worked long hours for little pay. Today, laws tell businesses that there is a certain amount they must pay workers. Machines today can do some work that people used to do. What do you think work will be like 100 years from now?

Times Change

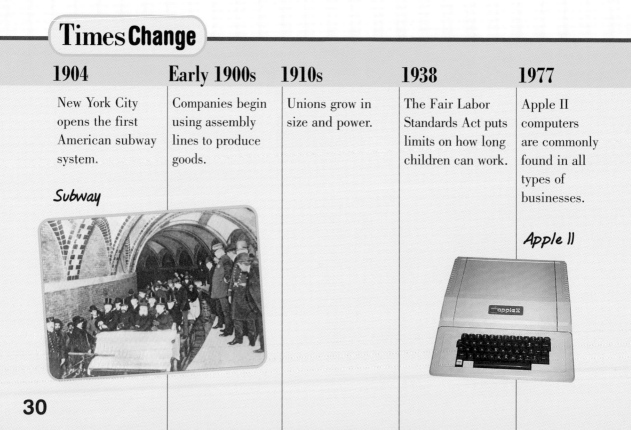

1904	Early 1900s	1910s	1938	1977
New York City opens the first American subway system.	Companies begin using assembly lines to produce goods.	Unions grow in size and power.	The Fair Labor Standards Act puts limits on how long children can work.	Apple II computers are commonly found in all types of businesses.

Subway

Apple II

Glossary

apprenticeship learning by experience with the help of skilled workers

automated when a machine runs by itself

blacksmith person who makes things out of iron

commuting traveling back and forth regularly

health insurance system that gives workers medical care

immigrant person who comes to a country to live

tailor person whose job is making or fixing clothes

telegram message sent by telegraph

telegraph machine that sends messages over wires by means of electricity

More Books to Read

Goldberg, Vicki. *Lewis W. Hine: Children at Work.* Prestel USA, New York, NY, 1999.

Ask an older reader to help you read these books:

Bartoletti, Susan Campbell. *Kids on Strike!* Houghton Mifflin Company. New York, NY, 1999.

Gourley, Catherine. *Good Girl Work.* Millbrook Press. Brookfield, CT, 1999.

Index